SPRING SNOW

John Charles McCue

Lovstad Publishing
Poynette, Wisconsin
Lovstadpublishing@live.com

ISBN: 0615753817
ISBN-13: 978-0615753812

Printed in the United States of America

Cover design by John D. Ahearn

DEDICATION

For many years I have kept this apology on the back burner. I have intended for years to write an apology to my relatives, friends and loved ones. The word "apology" should be taken in the sense of Plato's Apology as opposed to what has become the more commonly used definition of remorse or contrition. Webster's first definition of the word apology is:

A formal justification or defense.

Within the pages of this book lurks the Apology of John Charles McCue. As Plato attempted to explain and defend the actions of his mentor, Socrates, so I attempt to present the contents of these poems as an apology of my own views, feelings, peeves, pleasures, successes, failures, and philosophy.

After agonizing over whom to dedicate this work, I purposely decided to be vague. One might say, like Socrates, I chose the hemlock which could be considered the easy way out. I prefer to think that, like Hamlet's feigned madness, my method has been apparent to those who have ever known or loved me.

If I would try to enumerate all my relatives and friends, Murphy's Law would inevitably kick in causing me to omit someone. This would truly make me feel horrible. Goodness knows with the shape this world is in we all have enough to feel horrible about. So enjoy these works for what they are. It is my hope that you will draw inspiration and energy from some of these poems that will translate into action. All members of the human race must put aside their petty prejudices and learn to work together. Cooperation is no longer an option. It is absolutely necessary for the survival of our species.
John Charles McCue

Contact:
John McCue
P.O. Box 202
Bangor, WI 54614-0202
E-mail: goaliemcq1@msn.com
(608) 451-0039

What readers are saying about
SPRING SNOW

"These poems ring out with John McCue's voice of indignation against an unjust world. Not for the faint–hearted, these writings raise disturbing societal questions that many of us may not be willing to confront." *Gregory Wegner*

"John's Soccer Haikus took me back to 1950 when we defeated England 1-0."

Frank Borghi (right) Goalkeeper 1950 USA National Team and inductee into the National Soccer Hall of Fame and the St. Louis Soccer Hall of Fame.

"We will have been fortunate if we have had a chance to share in either John's skill as a soccer coach or as an honest and enthusiastic poet." *Jim Lafky*

"McCue's work is powerful. The strong and colorful images revealing the depths of his passion are tempered by unexpected and delightful flashes of humor." *Linda Fischer*

United States Army 1966 to 1968. Member of American Legion, Veterans of Foreign Wars (VFW), Disabled American Veterans (DAV), Viet Nam Veterans of America (VVA), Viet Nam Era Veterans (VEV) and AMVETS. Charter member of La Crosse branch of the NAACP.

Founder of the Veterans Opposing War (VOW)
and
People Opposing War (POW)

John McCue with Mike Miles at Fort McCoy, Wisconsin protesting Operation Desert Storm. December 1991.

26 June 07

It's been said that no person would wish for peace more than a soldier who has been to the field of battle. I've been to the field, and I have learned how to forgive my enemies. This would probably have never entered my mind and heart until I met you, John. Thank you so much for opening my eyes to a greater hope for our country and our world. I have been greatly honored to be a part of V.O.W. and your family. Through your wisdom, I will always affiliate myself and "my world" to place my body in the lives of people that do not advocate war. Why kill each other? We are only here for a short snap. Food and medicine only cost 10% of the price of ammo.

SFC. David Goodchild
Co. D. 2nd Bat. 173rd A-B-Bde 503 Inf.
Reg Viet Nam- November 1967 to June 1969

National King of the Hobos:
(Elected) 1990 at the National Hobo Convention in Britt, Iowa.

Poet Laureate of the Hobos for life:
(Dubbed) by King Roadhog USA in 1996.

Hobo nickname: "Songbird".

John, "Songbird" sings our National Anthem in Britt, Iowa with royalty from previous years. From far left to right: Queen Minneapolis Jewel; King Fishbones (from Maine); King Rambling Rudy (from Illinois); King Songbird; Queen Slow Freight Ben, and King El Paso Kid.

John played soccer as a goalkeeper at UMSL and UWGB.
He played first division amateur soccer in St. Louis, Missouri; Green Bay, Wisconsin; and Milwaukee, Wisconsin.

Played semi-pro soccer in Chicago, Illinois.
United States Soccer Federation (USSF) certified referee.
Holds a USSFD level coaching license.

Founder of the Bangor Soccer Club
President of the Coulee Region Soccer Club
Board Member of the
Wisconsin Youth Soccer Association (WYSA).

University of Missouri at St. Louis Soccer Team 1971
John McCue – back row, fourth from left

1966
1980
John McCue
1993
2006

John Charles McCue 1980
Photo by Merlin Thompson

John Charles McCue born in St. Louis, Missouri
June 5th, 1946 to Charles and Dorothy McCue
Education: St. Rita Grade School, 1960-1964
St. Louis U. High School and Normandy High School
Attended University of Missouri at St. Louis (UMSL)
and University of Wisconsin at Green Bay (UWGB)

Proud father of Jenifer, Amity, and Gavin.
Proud grandfather of Ethan, Corbin, and Mya (Jenifer).
Proud grandfather of Autumn (Amity).

Occupation: Retired bartender/Bouncer. Presently employed as a route driver, Sundance Photo, Jackson, Wisconsin for 22 years.

Hobbies: Singing, talking to strangers, and drinking beer (not necessarily in that order).

Vocation: Imagineer.

Amity & Dad celebrating Amity's 21st birthday

at Irish Fest, La Crosse, WI, 2006

Ethan, Jeni, Brian, Corbin
Mya

Autumn

Amity, Mike

The Holters

Foreword By John Medinger

"I have known big John McCue for a decade or more, with and without the chest-long beard. This "King of the Hobos" is a complex human being. He likes the simple things of life like a good drink and a good friend but he is also a man who has traveled around the block more than once. He understands the good side and the dark side of the human condition. He knows war but seeks peace. He will always befriend, as my Dad used to say, the "little guy."

He loves kids and soccer and gives generously of his time to both. He is not just a good guy but he gives out "Good Guy" awards each year at the Bangor "Hootenanny." I know because I received one.

John McCue writes well. He is an excellent wordsmith. This poetry is good stuff! You will like it. It is personal and powerful. It is a soul food for the heart and stimulation for the mind. For those people who have had a few hard knocks in your life, you will be able to identify with the emotions, imagery and events that are shared in these poems.

Buy this book. I guarantee that you will not be disappointed."

John Medinger, Former State Representative, Aide to Senator Russ Feingold and Mayor of La Crosse

Illustrator John Ahearn lives in St. Louis, Missouri and is a lifelong friend of author John McCue.

SPRING SNOW

AHE
ARN
06

CONTENTS

Author's Note:

Four poems have been added to this volume; *My Cup of Tea; The Mad Marsupial; Angevils;* and *Dust Off* can be found on the very last pages of this book.

Special Recognition and Awards:

The Second Coming found on page 4 won a monetary prize for 3rd place in a national open poetry contest sponsored by the Stockton Poetry Club of Stockton, California in 1986.

A Dozen Daisies found on page 53 won a monetary prize for 1st place (adult division) at the Hamlin Garland Days open poetry contest sponsored by the West Salem, Wisconsin Historical Society in the fall of 2009.

The Mad Marsupial found in the new section at the end of this book won 1st place (adult division) in a poetry contest sponsored by the John Bosshard Memorial Library in Bangor, Wisconsin to honor National Grouch Day on October 15th, 1997.

The Hobo found on page 9 was awarded a Bronze Medal at the 2011 National Veterans Creative Arts Festival; category: Solo Dramatic Poetry.

Dust Off* found in the new section at the end of this book was awarded a Gold Medal at the 2011 National Veterans Creative Arts Festival; category: Solo Inspirational Poetry. * Dust Off is the nickname given to the 498th Helicopter Ambulance Company that served in Viet Nam. We flew unarmed Hueys on medivac missions.

John McCue December, 2011

SPRING SNOW

ROYAL
PROCLAMATION

Let it be known throughout the land that as of this day "SONGBIRD" *who hails from* BANGOR, WISCONSIN *be recognized by the hobo community as having gained the title of* POET LAUREATE FOR LIFE. *Signed and sealed this date by the power invested in me at the National Hobo Convention at Britt, Iowa in August of 2002*

Dated MAY 26, 2003

"Red Bird Express"

Redbird Express
2002-2003 Hobo King

SPRING SNOW

TO BEGIN

To begin he flattered her –
Called her "Fancy Free."
He built her a fine statue –
Called it "Liberty."

He finally had her in his grasp
As she lay down in his bed.
With deception, lies, and promises
Her ego had been fed.
Dispensing then with gentle style,
Exploiting peak to foot;
He drained her of her vital fluid,
And covered her with soot.
He dug into her mountainside
Forcing wide the shaft.
Deeper he thrust his insensitive drill,
And all the time he laughed.
Deeper, deeper, deeper,
Until there burst a flood
Of sticky, slimy, salty sweat
And tons of human blood.
Deeper, deeper, deeper
Violating Mother Earth.
Through arrogant, shameful mockery,
He stripped her of her worth.

And now to this once virgin land
He's dealt the final blow –
He's pimped her out to others
So long considered foe.

EPITAPH

Write "today" on my gravestone
If it ain't much trouble, please,
Even if it's tomorrow
When my loved ones pay the fees.
'Cause I've always told them
As I went along my way –
It'll never be tomorrow.
I'll live and die today.

A naked soul's my only baggage
As I stroll down Shady Lane
'Cept for this pair of old walkin' shoes
That I'll use to board the train.
And when the devil makes his final bid
To rid me of my sorrows,
I'll tell him I'll stay in heaven today
And I'll meet you in hell tomorrow.

Oh, don't you lock me in a trunk
When you put me six feet under
'Cause Houdini's not my daddy's name
So I'll miss all the thunder.
And if I can get a message through,
You'll be the first to hear me say
My ETA for heaven
Will be sometime today.

Now, the Good Book's always told us
You're gonna reap just what you sow –
So be sure to plant a few seeds
To help your spirit grow.
And if you see one of your brothers
Confused and led astray,
You can pass him by tomorrow –
Just give him a hand today.

MY APARTMENT

Well, I moved into the apartment
After deciding to live alone.
I said to myself, "What the heck,
I'll have a place all of my own."

I started with the kitchen,
Waxed the floors and washed the pans,
Scraped the grease traps and defrosted the box.
It all went smoothly - according to my plans.

I moved into the living room
Vacuumed the rug and hung the drapes,
Arranged the dining table's centerpiece
With plastic bananas and sour grapes.

I pulled a police call on the can,
Wiped the tile and scrubbed the bowl,
Converted the tub into a shower,
Bought a dispenser with a double roll.

Posters, blacklights, woofers and tweeters –
Yep. The atmosphere was really neat.
But even the king-size waterbed
Didn't make my room complete.

All of a sudden it hit me right between the eyes.
What this lonely place could use
Is another pair of thighs,
With shapely hips and healthy lips
To get angry with over Freudian slips –
Someone to help me rearrange
The apartment's whole décor
From the dreamy, creamy ceiling
Down to the hardwood floor.

THE SECOND COMING

I knew it the day the hardware store
Ran a special on hammers and nails,
And bought up the whole Rock Island Line
To get the spikes from out the rails.

I knew it when the Chamber of Commerce
Parlayed all its funds
To buy the biggest arsenal
Of bombs and knives and guns.

Yep, I knew the second coming
Was right around the bend.
Yep, that fella Jesus Christ
Was gonna try again.

Sure enough, it happened
On a Tuesday morning.
Christ and some of his followers
Struck without a warning.

They hit the New York Stock Exchange
And dealt it a terrible blow
By jammin' the biggest ticker tape
With a beam from his bright halo.

Victoriously he paraded
With his troops down old Wall Street
While the winos, whores, and junkies
lined the curb to kiss his feet.

Then a mechanical cop was sent
As a token sacrifice.

With programmed politeness, summoned Jesus
To pay the permit price.

The savior turned with a loving gaze,
And the glance from his soft brown eyes
Blew the cop into a thousand bits
And scattered them to the skies.

Now Jesus turned to his followers
And beckoned not to falter.
"Very soon our passive blood
Will flow upon the altar."

Next, he turned to face the foe
And received the slings and arrows –
Calmly exchanged this first barrage
For bright red blood and yellow marrow.

When they brought the heavy guns
There only burst a fountain
of his precious, peaceful blood
That chased them up the mountain,

The last resort had finally come –
A magnate pushed the button.
But as the heavy casing fell
Christ absorbed it like a glutton.

Jesus made the sign of the cross,
And both sides' wounds were mended.
These were the last words that he said
As he gloriously ascended;
"Go now forever from this place of battle,
And let it be known to all for sure
That their overwhelming power to inflict
Fell short of our capacity to endure."

LONGING

The beauty of spring is enhanced by sounds.
Joyful shouts rise from all the playgrounds.
Busy birds chirp their age old song.
But my ears are deaf, and it all seems so wrong.
It all seems so senseless. Yes, spring's hard to bear
As long as I'm here and you're over there.

Summer is filled with some beautiful sights –
The bright sunny days, the moonlight drenched nights.
The sun and the moon surely must be –
But my eyes are blind, and these sights I can't see.
All summer brings to my eyes is a tear
As long as I'm here and you're over there.

Autumn sneaks in disguised by her shades
Of yellowredbrown as each and every leaf fades.
The days grow shorter. Every leaf has to fall.
As hard as I try, I can't understand it at all.
I'll never enjoy autumn's color fanfare
As long as I'm here and you're over there.

The grim face of winter wears a fearsome scowl
As the cold north wind begins to howl.
Winter is here – barren and bleak.
Everything dies when it reaches its peak.
With winter my life does surely compare
As long as I'm here and you're over there.

THE CISARNIVAL

Hurry, hurry, step right up!
We'll pour a matinee movie
In your coffee cup
So you can see a picture
Of a picture of the real thing.

Hurry up now, I ain't callin' you twice
To our soot belching factory
That makes your pollution device
So you can breathe a mixture
Of a mixture of the real thing.

But just stick with us on our twenty year plan.
Sure as you're born you'll die a million dollar man.
We'll buy you a plot up in Ketchikan
And hide your money from your children if we can.

Well, I see by the clock
It's time for sure
To conjure up a malady
And sell you a cure.
If you walk slow
We'll shoot penicillin in your toe.

Hurry, hurry, it's time to go!
We'll cut your grass for life
And even shovel your snow
So you can clearly see
How nature was meant to be.

Just buy a chance on our twenty year plan.
We'll mail you down south to get your pine box a tan
Pick you six pallbearers from the Ku Klux Klan.
We'll guarantee you'll never be an also-ran.

Songbird signing autographs at Britt, Iowa

John "Songbird" McCue was elected King of The Hobos in 1990 at Britt, Iowa. He received his name, "Songbird" from Hobo Bill (King of the Hobos, 1982) who said that when John sang, it sounded "like a songbird come down from the trees."

Song writer and singer, Jimmy Rodgers used the name Hobo Bill for his song, "The Last Ride of Hobo Bill."

THE HOBO

His old slouch hat was dusty –
His neckerchief white with salt.
He sang of things that happen to us all
That usually aren't our fault.
When he'd come to the part where the hurt began
He'd grow distant as he looked away and say,
"I've been coast to coast and rode 'em all.
Nothing seems to matter anyway."

He could yodel and moan like Jimmy,
And he picked like Jerry Reed.
Somehow you know that old slouch hat
And his guitar was all he'd need
To turn the people on –
To make us all feel high.
The son-of-a-gun knew every word
To McLean's "American Pie."

His message hit home as he sat erect
On that creaky old barstool.
Small talk and hustle soon gave way
To the wisdom of that old fool.
But as if to ask the question
Why are you listening to me?
When he came to that part that might bother us
His gnarled fingers slipped out of key.

Well, he rode his last song right on through.
And he didn't spare the pain.
He told us why a hobo's got to say goodbye
When he wakes up in the rain –
Somethin' about bureaucracy
1 2 3 and A B C.
It seems he's always on an outbound freight
Tryin' to reach you and me.

THE FARRAH FAWCETT FARCE

Hide down in your cellar,
Lock up your doors.
Batten down the hatches,
And don't let me catch you
Wearin' blue jeans with patches.
Excuse yourself when your sneeze,
And for heaven's sake, please,
Tighten up your ass
If you gotta pass gas.

Get with the program.
Take the 7:10 commuter.
Pay the high cost of living,
Or you'll jam the computer.
It's already been written
So don't you dare squawk
'Cause the Commies'll get us
If we're caught takin' a walk.
Oh, our secretary of state's
Got it figured for you feller.
All you gotta do is stay down in the cellar.

•

Go hide in the closet
With your Farrah Fawcett poster.
Get a grip on yourself, brother.
Raise your wine and toast her
'Cause her thirty-two teeth'll
Turn a Mona Lisa smile
After you've been inside
That closet for a while.
Just let the Farrah Fawcett farce
Make a stud of you, feller.
Just follow your nose back into the cellar.

Tune in next week –
Same time, same station.
Don't forget your coupon book
So you can get your ration.
The doctors shoot your valium
Directly through the cable
So you can start thinking
As soon as you're able.
We got a bald headed cop
Who's never wrong feller.
So just tell us who dunnit
And get back in the cellar.

PERFECT TIMING

I knew an old man
Who was made out a joke.
They say he was rich once
But died drunk and flat broke.
To this day I'm still baffled
Why his vagrancy's a crime an'
I'd say the old fella
Had pretty good timin'.

RAMBLINGS

Jesus was a carpenter.
Buddha was a bum.
Mahatma's daddy grabbed at his heart
When he heard what his little boy done.
Martin Luther King was just doing his thing
When the bullet went ping and zing went the strings
To a whole lot of things that Martin thought'd be cool.
And Lenny Bruce really weren't no fool,
While the rich got doctors to check their stools,
And somebody changed the golden rule
(So everybody'd think that he was cool).
Buried in the Village, Kahlil prophesied.
Joe shot Gerry and everybody died.
And all the onlookers' minds got fried,
While an ancient woman gave birth and cried
'Cause she knew her kid would be denied
The same way that they've always lied.
We'll put a freeze dried chicken in everybody's pot
With a television tube to make it hot
While we sit and watch our children rot.
We tell 'em it's their duty - they say it's not.
They get blown away on an army cot,
And the statistician says, "Thanks a lot!"

Whatever happened to Socrates?
I guess his questions blew away on a breeze.
Who the hell am I?
I don't know why.
All I can do is sit down and cry.
Watch the world go buzzin' by.
Hope some Seraphim really sing on high.
And keep on believin' I'll never die.

EMOTIONAL JAILBREAK

I should've known that someday it'd happen –
My feelings'd get sick and tired
Of bein' all dressed up real fancy
In the disguises I'd acquired.

But I still don't understand it,
Somehow it don't seem right
That so often true feelings get tried and fried
When exposed to a natural light.

So outa my mouth ran a feelin' one day
As naked as could be.
A big cop grabbed him, threw him in jail;
And then he threw away the key.

One mornin' fear ran outa my ear
Forgot his angry robe.
Got spooked by all the deafening noise,
And slipped offa my left ear lobe.

Once a little sorrow didn't wear any clothes,
Got up the gumption to drip outa my nose,
Stumbled head over heels offa my stiff upper lip,
But was luckily rescued by a Freudian slip.

Happy got slappy and decided to fly,
Hovered in my head 'til I opened my eye.
His wings froze up 'fore he got by my lash.
It was the coldness outside that caused him to crash.

MISTER PROFITEER

I just don't understand the actions,
Says Mr. Profiteer,
Of all these perverted, crumby factions.
Can someone tell me here?

I know the answer very well
Echoed a transparent voice.
Junkies, whores, and winos exist
Because they have no choice.

How can this be, in such a beautiful land
Where so many things are free?
Why do they abuse their welfare checks,
Unemployment, and ADC?

Because you've sold woman's desire
Of making love for fun.
Because you've tied up the harvest
And put the junkies on the run.

If you think for a moment
These problems are my doin',
I'll tell you now it's an inborn weakness
That takes them to their ruin.

You're the one who brought it up.
It's undoubtedly your fault.
The perpetrator of societal problems
Is locked in your greedy vault.

Dead bodies jam your money machine,
And now I'm afraid it's stalled.
While it seems your majestic bird of prey
Is getting a little bald.

You've whitewashed our banner so many times
The colors have run and faded
Until the spirit of '76
Is totally unrelated.

But you've the power to change it all –
Hire the men now to rechannel your riches
Instead of shrouding them in jungle fatigues
For their wakes in foreign ditches.

Allow all men to be completely free
As they choose to live out their lives.
Let them grow with their bouncing babies.
And make true love with their faithful wives.

Heed me, now, Mr. Profiteer!
Perhaps it's not too late
If we all join hands to redistribute your wealth
To avoid the inevitable fate.

John McCue and Vassar Clements

THE JESTER

He's got that all the time smilin'
Point of view.
He'd rather have it done unto him
Than see it done unto you.
He'll always make you happy,
Make you want to laugh and sing.
He seems to know how to soothe the hurt
That troubles always bring.

He's a gypsy. He's a hobo.
He's a jester. He's a clown.
He shoots his candid view of life
While hangin' upside down
He keeps his feet from gettin' burned
By dancin' round and round
And round and round and round and round
And round and round and round.

But there's a reason why he hides
Behind this picture that he paints you.
You're the only one who sees him cry
Whenever he feels blue.
So, it's your job that's hardest.
You've got to get him smilin' again.
You're a very well kept secret.
You're the jester's medicine

AHE
ARN
06

TIMES IS BAD

Times is bad.
Times is rotten.
This is the worst
That it's ever gotten.
Gotta keep tabs
On my toilet paper squares.
Might have to sell
Grandma's silverware.

The girl who's sittin'
In the driver's seat
Won't give me a kiss.
But she says I'm sweet.
Salvation, I'm told,
Comes in Cracker Jacks.
But if I look in the front
It'll be in the back.

My heart's been foreclosed,
I got the toe.
She said, "Don't come back
Without your ducks in a row."
I just got thrown.
And caught my foot in the stirrup.
I'm feelin' like an ant
In a fifth of maple syrup.

My window shield's
Gettin' covered with dirt,
And my wiper washer's
Gettin' low on squirt.
It's gettin' mighty hard
To find a person to touch.
Feel like a midget
Who can't quite reach the clutch.

I'm stuck in reverse
Drivin' next year's model,
Tryin' to rub a charley horse
Outa the throttle.
And when I get back
There'll be a helluva crash.
God help the poor film
That exposed 'fore the flash.

John McCue and Arlo Guthrie

THEY SAY HE'S CRAZY JUST BECAUSE

They say he's crazy just because
He'd rather watch an ice cube melt
Than stalk a defenseless animal
With a gun to make a furry pelt
To hang upon his wall
And brag on how he made it fall.

They say he's crazy just because
He'd rather live from day to day
Than give support to the local bank
To feed the loan sharks with his hard earned pay
Then discover dying that he's busted
While his insurance man's financially adjusted.

They say he's crazy just because
He'd rather take a Canadian fling
Than pimp his precious moral code
To defend the follies of the king
And collect some medals for his issued chest
That say he learned to kill the best.

They say he's crazy just because
He insists his freedom's his security,
And still can dig a pigtailed girl
Who clings steadfast to her purity
Who'll trust a hitchhiker even though he's male
And can lose four hours in a rummage sale.

So what if he doesn't kill for sport
Or nationalism's phony sway?
Can't justify a system
Where the money goes one way.
He'll always love that simple girl
Who's innocent and sweet,
Trusting, pure, and sensitive
Skipping freely through this phony world
In a pair of her own bare feet.

FLY NOW PAY LATER

Hey, Jack! I got a Cadillac
I can put you in for real cheap.
Just sign here. I'll buy you a beer.
The time is near for you to get a good night's sleep.
It's only had one owner
Who only drove it a little.
Almost made it to the suburbs.
They called him Y. T. Middle.
I'm tellin' you the truth, Mr. Black.
I can get ol' Y. T. offa your back.
If you'll just sign here, I'll buy you a beer.
Have no fear.
The time is near for you to get a good night's sleep.
Pleased to meet you Mr. Red.
My real name's Abe.
But you can call me Fred.
Why don't you trade in that ol' Pontiac?
I'll garnishee the clothes
Right off your papoose's back.
Have no fear. Just sign right here.
The time is near for you to get a good night's sleep.
I'll buy you a beer. I'll throw in a mirror.
It's got all kinda gears.
It'll smear any other car on the road.

Now that old Cadillac just sits still
While those three people pay its bill.
They drove in and out
While they were laughed about.
By the man standing up on the hill.

MAVERICK

From cowboy hats, pintos, and ponies
Now he carries an I.D. that's phony.
A new mechanized cowpoke,
One of the unbranded young folk,
He should've been born years ago.

He rides point on the guard rails
Like his daddy rode fences,
And his poor mother wonders
When he'll come to his senses.
He should've been born years ago.

The Dirt Band plays "Mr. Bojangles"
As he hits the outskirts of Durango,
Rollin' as fast as he can
In his beat up old customized van.
He should've been born years ago.

But he'll never know as the years start to show
That he's always been on the wrong track.
When he gives up his raidin' and his sunsets start fadin,'
He'll find out he's been on the way back.

SPRING SNOW

Spring snow clings to his shoulders
And cannot melt.
In stubborn defiance of thermal laws
It weaves a priceless pelt.
Its crystal clear persistence
Tells his story well—
So far removed from the mundane arts
It refuses to melt in hell.
On flames consuming tons of flesh
Fall empathetic flakes of despair
From hexagon shaped, bright, brown eyes
Ablaze in a frigid stare
Frozen on the fiery haze
And loved ones writhing there.

NATIVITY

As I plunge to my death by you,
And your limbs shiver with your suicide by me;
We share the same fantasy that eclipses
The evasive light that is fruitlessly filtered
By the eye.
Conceived is hope – the conception of desire.
But its manifestation is not for the living.
Cold, stiff, eternally strong is the grip that knots
The umbilical cord.

John McCue and Tom Paxton

THE PENSION PLAN

Pension plans are a gamble,
And I'm not a gamblin' man.
I make my draw on a Friday
And spend it as fast as I can.
Saturday mornin' may find me
Broke and missin' a shoe –
All sprawled out on the kitchen floor
Wondrin' where I am and who's who.

I knew an old duffer on the pension plan;
Now all he can raise is his cane.
His checks compared to what they promised him
Are just about to drive him insane.
Yup, the pension plan's made him nervous
With managerial/labor disputes.
After thirty-seven years in their service,
They screwed him out of his loot.

I just turned thirty-one years old;
Aint worrying about thirty-two.
If Dow Jones crashes to the bottom
I don't intent to turn blue.
'Cause the Gates, the Perots, and the hoboes
I've always considered the same,
And if I die later on today,
I'll be way ahead of the game.

I shoot the bull with my ol' bartender
While he pours me my souvenirs.
I have a ball gettin' naked
Just to hear all the derelicts cheer.
You can laugh at me real hearty
When I fall down on my face.
But I swear and be damned I'll haunt you
If you bury me in diamonds and lace.

Spend your money just as fast as you can.
Don't gamble on the pension plan.
Have a real good time while you're in your prime.
It may be all over soon.
They'll use your money to go to the moon,
Oil their war machine and their marching tune.
Gamblin'll surely take you to your ruin.

John McCue and John Prine

A TAXI DRIVER'S DREAM

A taxi driver's dream
Is a long legged,
Painted lady fair
With a bottle of booze
And an I don't care.
A purse full of dough
And a wherever you go.
You see, I'm stood up
And prime for the kill.
When this soldier's dead
We'll get a refill.
Relax and unwind–
Enjoy all my pleasure.
Be easy and smooth –
Your pace at your leisure.
For when you awaken
All that's in store
Is a smart aleck kid
Who likes slammin' the door,
A demanding old hag
Mouth reeking of bagel
Who over a nickel
An hour will haggle,
A cool young dude
Who spews the hack jargon
Just tryin' to get
His ride at a bargain,
A four year old kid
Who just shit his pants,
Somebody's out of town
Uncles and aunts,
A traffic cop who doesn't like cabbies,
A cranky dispatcher,
And a thousand dear Abbies.

If the boss ever decides
To be so blatantly cruel,
And declares the daydream
Against company rules,
I swear and be damned
On a stack of street guides,
Little men in white coats
Will be givin' me rides.

"Mountain Dew," "Frypan Jack," Author "Songbird."

FLASHBACK CASUALTY

Well, that night everybody in the neighborhood
Glued their eyes to the Ten O'clock News
Just to see how the ol' salt got it
And to hear all of the witnesses' views.
The ol' colonel bronzed his combat boots
And hung 'em in his car.
He'd just pulled out of the parking lot
And he hadn't gone too far
When his right front tire decided to blow
And he swerved in front of a van.
Got nailed by a local hard rock group,
Ran upside the curb, and scraped his pan.
The drummer said, "I'll check the damage."
As he followed where the tire marks led,
And when he came back he was white as a ghost.
He said, "I think the ol' guy's dead."
The driver told the mini-cameraman,
"I don't know why the colonel's dead.
I didn't hit very hard,
And them boots just bumped his head.
But right before I smacked him
He glanced in his rear view mirror
Yelled into his c.b. radio –
His eyes were glazed with fear."
A local amateur radio buff
Told of a call on channel two,
"His radio procedure was very poor –
His voice just come out of the blue.
Whatever it was he was hollerin' about
Didn't come through too clear –
Somethin' about a broken right flank
And they're overrunnin' our rear."

And now for a recap of today's events:

It looks like good weather's on the way back.
and Hawkes, John L., Colonel, U.S.M.C., retired,
died of a heart attack.

AMNESTY

Jesse, can't you see
Why I hitch these highways?
Jesse, I've got to be free.
Meet me at the caverns
For a change of horses,
And we'll ride again –
You, Frank, and me.

But, Jesse, it's real important to me
That all the killin' be through.
It's the only way I can justify
Carryin' on for you.
A righteous cause can never be forgiven
For the spilling of innocent blood.
We've got to stop now, and patch up our differences
With Missouri clay and Mississippi mud.

Jesse, the big day's a comin'
And way long overdue –
That glorious day we've been waitin' for,
Me, Ma Samuels, and you.
But gunplay's not the answer –
There's a harder but better way.
Got to smother trouble in our outstretched arms
Each and every day, Jesse, it's the only way.

Hush, now, can't you hear
That old Cannonball rumblin' by?
Can't take no dead weight,
So, Jesse, open your heart,
And we'll catch her on the fly.

SWEET CORN

The sweet corn's comin' up.
It's the sweetest I ever ate.
Reckon we best harvest it
Before it gets too late.
And Johnny Mendoza swam
Way cross the Rio Grande
Where he was met by the sheriff –
Paid his life for the tariff.
Crazy spic, that's what he gets
For goin' against the grain
And pickin' on me
'Cause whoever I get in my sights I see
A dead man who can't brother me.
Well now, the beans are a sproutin'
Made Grampa stop his poutin'.
Look's like the crop's a bumper
Best oil the belt and pump 'er.
Chief Half Eagle
Sat on his reservation
While a lawyer stole his land
Through political conversation.
They cut off his water
'Cause they said there was a shortage.
Built a big steel bridge
And sunk pilings in his portage.
Now the chief sits on his island
And guzzles cheap wine,
But the sweet corn's comin' up.
It's gonna work out fine.

DA DA DA DA	**DA DA DA**	**DA DA**	**and**	**DA**
poochy bellies	little tits	nice butt	and	legs
tin can kicking	scuffed up shoes	scolded	and	spanked
high school degrees	mortar rounds	caskets	and	flags
painted faces	panty hose	hairspray	and	junk
derelicting	dawn drinking	locked up	and	flogged
cocktail waitress	pinched her butt	bounced out	and	barred
bartender bull	pushin' drinks	blended	and	drunk
battered buddies	frozen eyes	limp limbs	and	dead

Poet John McCue, 1993

FAT CAT

The biggest fat cigar smokin' cat
Will change to an innocent child.
And the twelve year old junkie
Who's forced to carry a gun
Will no longer have to
Rob, kill, and run.
The changes'll come
And no one'll notice.
The buzzing of machinery'll
Be given back to the locust.
The sly opportunists
Who collect for god's sake
Will be buried forever
And no longer take.
Teachers of controlled learning'll
Be flunked out of college
While stomachs that are yearning'll
Be fed with true knowledge;
And those who start wars
For their own fame and power –
From destructive, cold, hail stones –
To soft, misty spring showers.
If you don't think
This ever can happen
Just lie down with me
And we'll take a nap an'
When we wake up
If the world's still the same
We'll burn it all down
With Promethean flame.
When the smoke and the stench
Of the conflagration does rise
We'll let hearts who are loving
Try the world on for size.

HYPOCRISY

I'm sick and tired of hearing about
Jesus of Nazareth –
The infallible boss.
I'd rather have known him
When he was down and out
And nailed upon the cross.

It's hard to believe
That those three hours
He hung in his blood and tears
Have become so
Blasphemously perverted
For the past two thousand years.

The pitch is very clever
As steeples scrape the heavens
Atop martyred bricks
Of the very rarest sort
Leaving the sheep
Pinned in a crucial fix.

The latest chip off Peter's rock
Spews such pious precepts
As greed will cast you into Hades
While he's donned with
Beautiful jewels and satin
And chauffeured in a new Mercedes.

Christ's sharp words of truth
Have dulled in meaning
Since ignorance reamed hollow.
While it's the apathy of Pilate
And the echoes of the mob
That we've been tricked to follow.

Author John McCue and Chris Bielski
Playing for strikers at Weyerhaeuser Paper Co. in St. Louis, MO, 1980

Folksinger Larry Penn and Author John McCue
At Songbird's Annual Hootenanny in Bangor, WI, 1990

WALLS AND OTHER WINDOWS

While staring through my wall one day
I began to feel a strange compassion for it.
I thought, poor wall, through the years you've been
Dug under, leapt over, circumvented, and leveled.
But no one stops to talk.
Who are you, Wall?
Is it your nature to inhibit mobility or to inspire creativity?
As you held Henry in your midst.
Did you shackle him
Or did you fashion wings for his spirit
With nothing to lose in flight
But the staticity of his corporeal extension?
As Martin's coal black face peered out of his cage
Into the blinding white abyss, did his peaceful brown eyes
Take to the seclusion of the darkest reaches of his mind,
Or did you catapult them to splatter the creamy shroud
With an indelible stain that will eternally endure?
Could Jesus be bound by perpendicular planks
While his body and spirit lie in parallel lines
Only to wave to one another across the way?
Was his spirit choked by anguish
Or was it freed by the executioners of his body?
Do we die of heartbreak over the death of a dear friend,
Or is our heart strengthened by the sinews of his memory?
John and Bobby were born within the walls of wealth
But put to sea with the perpetual abundance of their spirits
As their only provisions, casting their Neptunic ideals freely
Into the abyss of true life. Was Socrates' hemlock a stagnant,
Polluted pool incapable of reflection or a wide rolling sea
Of which he saw his spirit borne on high sail?
I ask you, Wall, did Moses strike you twice in lack of faith
Or did the conflict of body and spirit emerge in nervous
Vibration which stuttered his staff instead of allowing it
To touch you calm and true?

As evening creeps my daily
Candle burns low and this darkness on you, Wall, only
Confounds me more. So, I shall pass to the realm of my
Illuminating dreams and absorb the blows of my
Unconscious mind as it struggles to free itself
From the chains of my fearful consciousness
So good night, Wall, and thank you for a therapy session
My vanity glass could never afford.

Hobo Queens "Lump" (left), Slo Freight Ben (right), And John "Songbird" McCue

REVERIES ON THE ROCKS

The little girl across the street… Flying a kite…
Sleigh riding… Skating… Flashlight tag… Ghost shows…
Soapbox derbies... Lemonade stands…The
street car tracks—look both ways… Water balloon fights…
Hey, Tommy, let's crawl down the sewer… Wipe your
feet… A dime a tooth!... The tree house…The tire
swing… Tommy swallowed a penny… Hey, Eddie,
let's put a penny on the railroad tracks… Baseball flips…
Mumbley peg… Dig a foxhole before the Japs get us. ..
You be the Japs. Aw, I'm always the Japs… Don't
step on cracks (unless you're mad)… It's ten minutes
'til two-thirty…The snowman… Candy cigarettes…Pull
Mom's dress and point to cookies… Lick the icing
spoon… Jaw breakers—what color is it now?... Freddy
cried 'til his mommy came…Valerie…The teacher
hates me… I like recess and lunchtime the best…The
big slide… BB gun fights or you're chicken…The big
kids threw our ball over the fence… Pop's home, Mom…
Kiss… Clarabell talks with his horn… a two foot icicle…
The dog that "followed" me home… The jungle gym…
How do you play Tippy?... Betcha can't put out the
street light from here… six "Our Fathers" and six "Hail Marys"…
Over the fence on a bounce is only a double…
Is four of a kind good, Pop?... Here to the fence and
back and the loser has to ask her - wanna play spin the
bottle?... I think I'll play goalie… Wow, a bicycle…
Danny's my partner – we're altar boys… Wash behind
your ears… Say your prayers… Wait 'til I get big…
The paper route… I dare ya – I double dare ya.
Oh, yeah? – Yeah!... Hank's lawn mower…
Lightning bugs… Hide and seek… Gary's the
best tree climber… Wigwam broke his leg slidin'…
Rhino's the best catcher… Sked's the best all
around… Gragnani joined the army…

Cookie's the prettiest – No she ain't – Yes she is – No she
ain't – Wanna fight?... Pool chalk on my shirt…
Snow forts… On the rocks … Sked's a pro soccer
player… Seventeen stitches… Gary's a cop… Eddie
died of cancer… So'd Hank… Hangovers … Rhino
was a full flash Green Beret… Tie my shoe, Mom…
A new barmaid… Wigwam died in a car crash a
week after graduation… Tuck me in, Mom…
Freddie's kids cry when he's gone… Danny's
married – so's Cookie… Danny's divorced…
Wanna flip for the break?... Gragnani got
Killed in the Nam-Fuck!!
Gimme a double… You're getting a spanking…
The little girl across the street moved away …

LAST CALL FOR ALCOHOL! Drink up, pal,
I gotta close this joint… Don't get smart with me…
What the hell's eatin' you anyway?

Sam Day and Author John McCue at Ft. McCoy

BOOGIE WOOGIE

When I've had it with the boss
And I'm sick and tired
Smack dab in the middle
Of crawlin' and fired,
I punch out his clock
And saunter downtown
Wave my hat, hoot and holler,
Plant my boots on the ground,
And I boogie, boogie woogie woogie woogie.
My baby meets me there
Cause she's had a bad day.
She wants me to comfort her
So, what can I say?
I grab her gently by the shoulder
And we jump in the line
As she sways and she twirls
Whoa, she's lookin' so fine
And she boogies, boogie woogie woogie woogie,
When they shut off the music
And the others start to roam,
We jump into out pickups;
And race each other home.
We're gonna kick back
Gonna have a good night
I slip the key in the lock
And she blows out the light.
And we boogie, boogie woogie woogie woogie.

HYPE

The first thing you do before you buy it
Is squeeze it, wind it up, and try it.
If it's an aeroplane, you fly it.
If it's a crowbar, try to pry it.

A baseball team had a new recruit.
He was thirty feet tall
So they put him by the wall
And dared all the batters
To try to knock it out of the park.
Well, they all tried to go to the opposite side,
But they struck themselves out,
And it hurt their pride.

Then a little skinny guy
With a big hook nose
Dug in his feet
And said, "Here goes."

He hit a lazy fly ball –
Bounced off the giant's head
Fell into the bleachers –
The coach turned red.

On the Star of the Game Show
The little guy explained,
"I'm a natural pull hitter
So I decided not to yield.
And besides
In all of the hullabaloo
The big guy never did prove
That he knew how to field.

BUSTED UP OLD VETERAN

Yep, he slings that pint in his pocket
Like a pistol on his hip,
And there ain't no faster story
Than the one shot from his lip.
That man can tell some tales
You ain't never heard before.
He'll leave you with your mouth hangin' wide open
As he stumbles out the door.

He's proud of his three piece, custom made,
Jade inlaid pool cue.
He won it in an all night poker game
Aboard ship in '42.
Now it's his only visible means of support –
His only claim to fame.
His haggard old eyes still sparkle
Every time he wins a game.

The rich people say he's worthless
His kinfolk think he's a fool
The way he carries on at his age
Playin' poker and shootin' pool.
But I never saw him hurt nobody,
And he don't owe me a dime.
He's just a busted up old veteran
Out of step and out of time.

He's a busted old veteran,
Out of step and out of time.
As he staggers out of rhythm,
Numbered days seem out of rhyme.
And you can't quite put your finger on it
No matter how you try.
But there's something good as gold about him
That just won't be denied.

Now he's all mixed up about wartime
Says his nephew's gone or his niece.
Can't figure why folks are always fightin'
Instead of workin' together for peace.
Sometimes his flag lies limp and ashamed.
Sometimes it makes him feel proud.
I reckon he'll just keep on bein' himself –
Rollin' and drinkin' and thinkin' out loud.

CAESAR VINCET

Although very subtle,
Caesar's victory is sweet.
It's been two thousand years
Since someone last kissed my feet.
The soldier bowed his head.
The sun was ashamed.
The heavens spoke thunder
And called out my name.

If I could've only died once
All alone on that hill,
It would've been such a relief,
But I'm hangin' there still.
The sweat burns my eyes
Over and over again
Each time you are cold
And turn out a friend.

My beard's long and gray,
Sandals are worn out and stink.
Sour grape wine
Is my favorite drink.
I'm fed up with pompous,
Golden idols, and silk
While the suburbians still thrive
On the ghetto's sweet milk.

CONCRETE AND STEEL

Concrete, clay, steel and iron
Consort together to control my mind.

Clay under concrete, iron made to steel,
Underlying components to control my will.

Concrete is hard, steel is strong,
Making it difficult not to go wrong

If my mind is to see it has to look
Past the apparent into every far nook.

To properly function my will has to try,
And that can be accomplished by just asking, "Why?"

My observant mind and discriminating will
Refuse to be crushed by concrete and steel.

THE BOA CONSTRICTOR

The boa can move without a leg,
and it's big enough to eat an ostrich egg.

The ostrich egg can't realize
The atrocious way in which it dies.

The death of a man is different I think,
For every one killed has raised quite a stink.

But the stench is subdued by sweet scents we smell,
And the one who sprinkles them will never tell.

THE FEARLESS HUNTER

The fearless hunter sees everything.
No game escapes his eye.
Plotting, tracking, stalking, killing
Innocent prey – so still they lie.

Some will pick the carcass clean –
Use the hides to warm their beds
Others for Salome's dance
Will offer up the heads.

While the deer, prince of the forest green,
Takes only for his need
Grazing harmlessly into forever
Diana's prancing steed.

At last he'll see his reflection
In a telescopic lens
He'll feel what paranoia is
He'll know oblivion.

Drawing by Amity McCue

BURROS AND COWBOYS

Thank goodness there's still cowboys
Ridin' roundups to draw their pay –
Shootin' their whiskey straight up in the saddle –
Star gazin' where they lay.
Roarin' through town on Saturday night,
They kick and they snort and they bray.
Thank goodness there's still cowboys
To help the burros have somethin' to say.

Dodgin' them bullets and duckin' the law,
Weary from the chase but still quick on the draw,
Boxed in a canyon, cut off at the pass,
Odds are against them. How long can they last?

Well, we watched the slaughter of baby seals
While their mamas sat and cried.
We chased Big Blue all around the ocean
'Til he rolled right over and died.
We catered to the whims of the tourists,
Believed the politicians when they lied.
But burros and cowboys are much too stubborn
As off to the border they ride.

FOR JENIFER

I've run over the hills.
I took a few pills.
I felt the chill of the valley.
Fought my way out of the alleys.
And here I am now
At the foot of the mountain –
Looks like a septic tank
About to spout a fountain.
But I've got to climb up it.
Come hell or high water
So someday some poor fellow
Can look straight at his daughter
And say, "With every new day
I'll love you a little bit more,
And you know I've a strange feeling
That I've seen you before."

Liam Clancey and John McCue, 2006 Irish Fest,
LaCrosse, Wisconsin

FOR TOMMY RYAN

In those early years
We ran and played
On baseball diamonds
And soccer fields.
We were often
Roman soldiers
With wooden swords
And cardboard shields.

So long Puff
And Jackie Paper.

Mom's garters that held
Our shin guard's up
Finally fell
For ponytails.
Never mind, now,
Uncle Sam's a callin,'
And we're just
As tough as nails.

Goodbye SLUH
And CBC.

The stars were taken
Out of the windows
As we double-stepped
Out of line.
It was time for us
To have some fun –
Kiss those girls
And spill some wine.

Take care
Mom and Dad.

While Danny and I
Are still hung up
On soccer
And such trivial things,
Butch's hands are busy
Forever taping up
Sprained angels' wings.

God's first team
Is calling me.

UNDER PAR

So what's the average fellow got that I ain't got?
I get to watch the moon all night –
That is, when it's out and shining bright.
Ain't puttin' him down. He likes life,
And I think that's real nice.
But please don't knock my wanderin' ways
'Til you've seen the same sunset twice.

So what's the average Joe got that I ain't got?
No more belongins, I suspect.
The bank owns his home, and do they collect!
Sure he's got his wife and kids
Lined up all in a row.
But I see my child in every kid's face
No matter where I go.

I've never objected to nature
Rather that protocol being my guide.
You see, I toss in my sleep so sundown
And sunup come on the same side.
So what's the average guy got that I ain't got?
General consensus, I'm afraid, that's all.
Forgive me, I must be running along –
The wind just gave me a call.

A DOZEN DAISIES

One for the long green stem that's buried in the earth,

One for the clinging leaf that hangs on for all it's worth,

One for the snow white petal and your sweet purity,

One for the golden center burning to be free,

One that awakens at every dawn to drink the morning dew,

One to close at Sol's retreat to mark the day is through,

One that droops so heavy when nothing will go right,

One that's in your smile's sparkling rainbow light,

One that kissed me, one that won't,

One that hides beneath the rest,

One that doesn't fit, can't be arranged–

The one I love the best.

COMPUTER MUTANT

Want a job in computers,
So you can go from
Real
To
Reel?
Get a good job selling people.
Give the tapes the right to
Steal.
Keep a lookout for the one in
Red,
So you can repossess his
Bed.
Just hope the track get stuck
When it's your turn to be de
ad
dea
d
ead
d e

Dead!

THE DONKEY

Our newsletter
Comes out of the basement
Sad but true that's the way that it is.
It seems in every pull
When they're through with the donkey
They shred the carrot,
And claim it's not his.
It's not his what he pulled for.
It's no longer his why he died,
They've taken away
What he believed in.
Now he asks himself, "Why?"
Why did I try when they called me?
Why do I try
Though it's done?
'Cause I'm glad
That my war is over
But I'm sad
That yours has begun.
I'm sad that yours has begun.
For my money you can stand up
Or run.
Just don't forget
When it's over
No one'll remember
How it had begun.

HOOKED

See him walkin' down the road
With his back pack hangin' on a heavy load,
Playin' hide and seek with the railroad tracks,
Getting' lots of static, just lookin' for some slack.

Lookin' for a job, ain't no bum.
But somebody's got to go and come.
Playin' one legged hop scotch over highway cracks,
Got a kink in his neck tryin' not to look back.

He was a hobo when he got here,
He'll be a hobo when he goes.
In the winter he heads for the sunshine.
Come summer he'll be where it snows.
Loneliness lines his pocket book,
No money to be found.
But like a bad penny or a rainbow,
Ever so often he comes around.

"I'm gonna quit it all someday!"
I heard him shoutin' as he limped away,
wavin' his walkin' stick at the sky,
As he caught that ol' Cannonball on the fly.

John McCue cir 1980. On the road in Florida.

THE UNCERTAIN BEAT

Dancing to the uncertain beat of a drum –
they never really know the reason they've come.

Not really knowing the reason they came,
The boy plays the role –
The girl plays the game.

Being uncertain, they start to explore.
Discontent with a little, they always try more.

Reality exhibits itself in a child.
The girl become a woman,
The young boy goes wild.

A few years later their kid's turn comes
To go out to parties and dance to the drums.

King of the Hobos, John "Songbird" McCue
Oktoberfest parade, La Crosse, WI, 1991

THE HOBO WHITTLER'S DREAM

He envisions a hobo jungle
Down at the railroad museum.
The hoboes will come from miles around
All the kids will get to see 'em.

Adolph's got his jackknife out,
And the world's gonna give him some wood.
You know he's all the time creatin' things
That no one thought he could.

He'll whittle you a ball-in-a-cage
Right before your eyes,
And slide it up a neckerchief he'll give you
Much to your surprise.

The whittler just needs a piece of wood
Big as a railroad museum,
So he can carve a hobo's heart
Big enough for kids to see him.

Written by John Mc Cue in tribute to the artistry of Adolph Vandertie, and dedicated to Adolph and his wife, Adeline.

Adolph's hobo art can be seen at the Aswaubenon Historical Museum in Green Bay, Wisconsin.

LOVE

The most repressed word in the world is "love".
That's because love don't make no money.

There are parking meters downtown
'Cause people hate to walk.
There are cell phones
'Cause people hate to talk.
There are sleeping bags
'Cause people hate to stay.
There are king-size beds
'Cause people hate to go away.
There's beer
'Cause people hate to think.
There's purple
'Cause people hate pink.

But, if you love,
It's got to be for free,
And I've got to give it to you,
Even if you don't give it to me.

John McCue and Richie Havens

TRICKS WITH TIME

Only if you wipe away the nostalgic tear
That blurs the past
And simultaneously focus the
Much distorted future,
Can you capture the fleet-footed inventor of both.

The past is what it will be.
The future is what it was.
The present is what it is.
Happiness never was and never will be.

The present-ah, what a scamp!
By the time you figure where he'll be–he was.

HIDDEN HUNGER

When your eyes and nose are numb to spring
You'll never really learn a thing.

Seize the moment. Hold the hour.
Behold the sunset. Smell the flower.

Enjoy the privilege of living to day
Instead of wishing your life away.

For if you don't before you're dead
Your greatest hunger will have gone unfed.

MARIAH

Yawa s
l
r
u
c
r
he
Throwing her eyes at me as gs
in
she sw

fooling her bell bottoms as she stops
and they g o
g
n
i
p
Scarf flip in mid-air

i p i g
shawl r p l n from the shock
earringstinklin
beads clattering
shoelaceflapping

o g n n
Surgin greceding w i g leaving
d d i g e v
a

John & Boxcar Willy, 1984

Steam Train Maury Graham & John, 1985

ONCE UPON A TIME ON THE WAY TO A COTTAGE ON THE LAKE

In the land of snow
When the sun was high
Two spirits free collided
While flying for the sky.

At Frost's unchartered crossroads
Where life's pure water springs
Where the heather is forgiving
And the frisky bluebird sings.

Their broken wings were mended
By new old friends they found
Who easy spent their treasures
And spread them all around.

No longer flying solo
Now soaring hand in hand,
Their spectres just a wisp behind,
To a peaceful verdant land.

Immersed safe in the garden
Their presence sparsely known
They set about to building
An earthly home their own.

Her loyal curtsy makes them three
He bows and they are four
And the musty raven changing tune
Doth quoth, "Forevermore."

Symbols sudden clashing
Minders of reality
Oft find them hanging on the edge
Twixt hopeless and serenity.

And though he sometimes bobbles
Tired eyes slide off the ball
He strives to keeps his promise
To catch her if she falls.

"Alas!" the rusty hinges shrieked
Bemoaning the razing choice
Like the heart stopping, stabbing sound
Of a scolding mother's voice.

At last the raven sunk to gloomy
Calls it back and quite clear to me
As he paces o'er the creaky floor.
His crippled gait a harsh reminder
That only in my dreams I'll find her,
And there's no use in hoping anymore.

Oh, cruel fate that lives to shatter
All my dreams and all that matter
On bloody knees I beg you to restore.
Of you I desperately implore.
The heartless answer froze me to the core.
Quoth Poe's bastard raven, "Nevermore."

THE TEN THAT MOSES BROKE IN ANGER*

1. Love god
2. Speak of god
3. Come together and enjoy god and creation
4. Love those who begat you
5. Procreate
6. Know one mate
7. Give
8. Speak well of your neighbor
9. Love your neighbor
10. Appreciate your neighbor's work

*WHO SAYS THE SECOND SET OF COMMANDMENTS WERE THE SAME AS THE FIRST SET? *(The debate is not ended yet.)*

Music elicits the wide spectrum of emotions that all humans share. When fingers caress its keyboard, the piano cares not what color they are, whether they are smooth or calloused, feminine or masculine. The piano cares not whether those fingers ever fold in prayer. If they do, the piano cares not to Whom they pray.

Musical instruments see for the blind, hear for the deaf, and sing for the mute. Through the ages, many musicians have used their instruments to compensate for their handicaps—freeing their spirits and touching our souls.

Music is truly the international language. What mother has not hummed her babe to sleep with a lullaby native to her land? Music needs no translator. When music complements lyrics it facilitates their translation. The Veterans Opposing War (VOW) believe that musicians who ignore political boundaries, challenge tyranny (foreign or domestic), and advocate for the impoverished and abused serve their respective countries far better than myopic, power appointed diplomats and ambassadors.

So, let's raise a toast! "Here's to the minstrels, troubadours, and composers who stir our imaginations, tear down the walls of ignorance, and give succor to the less fortunate. Verily, they are the Robin Hoods and Maid Marians of the arts!"

Inspiration for this monument was drawn from two songs: "Imagine," written and performed by John Lennon; and "Ebony and Ivory," written by Sir Paul McCartney and performed by Sir Paul and Stevie Wonder. This monument symbolizes the hope that the people of all lands will someday learn to live in harmony with one another and the earth. "You may say I'm a dreamer but I'm not the only one. I hope someday you'll join us and the world will live as one." *John Lennon*

The piano was made by Doug Flahaut at Allied Steel in Rockland, Wisconsin, and painted by KKID Custom Painting of Mindoro, Wisconsin. All plaques were made by PAT Line of Bangor, Wisconsin. All plaque support posts were made and donated by Gene Schaller of Bangor. The flora is donated, planted and kept up annually by Mark and Kay Kastenschmidt of Bangor.

The monument was dedicated by Senior Class members and staff of the Bangor High School Band and Choir in concert with the Hootenanny crew on Sunday May 24, 2009. It can be viewed at the Village Park in Bangor, Wisconsin.

(Photos, pages 67, 68, 69 by Jeff Cozy)

SOCCER MONUMENT

Association football, commonly known as soccer, is the most popular team sport in the world. The number of countries where it is played exceeds the number of countries that belong to the United Nations. Because of its universality, the Veterans Opposing War (VOW) believes that soccer can be used as a tremendous galvanizing force throughout the world to promote peace. Many countries are involved in cultural exchange programs through soccer. Through these programs understanding is enhanced, and unfounded fears are allayed. Cultural myths are demystified. Religious differences are tolerated. This monument to the game of soccer symbolizes the hope that the youth of the world who come together today to share in a friendly game of soccer will become the leaders of tomorrow who will learn to share the world.

The monument in Village Park, Bangor, Wisconsin, was dedicated on the Sunday of Memorial weekend in 2003 by Harry Keough, a member of the 1950 USA National Soccer Team. That team defeated England by the score of 1 to 0 in the biggest upset in Soccer World Cup history. Mr. Keough is a member of the National Soccer Hall of Fame in Oneonta, New York.

This project could not have been completed without the generosity of the people of Bangor, and soccer clubs throughout the Coulee Region.

(Photo by S. Arthur)

SIGNIFIGANCE OF THE THREE FLAGS

The white flag with green trim flying at the top is that of The Veterans Opposing War (VOW).

Just below the VOW flag flies the flag of the nation whose men currently reign as Soccer World Cup Champions.

Below that flies the flag of the nation whose women currently reign as Soccer World Cup Champions.

The flags were first raised in the summer of 2006. At that time the respective Champions were Italy's Men and Germany's women.

In the event that either the men or the women of the United States of America would reign as Soccer World Cup Champions, the United States of America flag would fly above all others out of respect for national flag etiquette.

(Photo by S. Arthur)

West Salem Jr. Varsity Soccer Team – Fall of 2003

SOCCER HAIKUS

SOCCER
The beautiful game
Most popular in the world
Game of the people

GOALKEEPER
All alone bright quick
Fearless a bit off center
Defender's best friend

DEFENDER
Staunch and relentless
Building up and destroying
Goalkeeper's best friend

MIDFIELDER
Defend and attack
Running giving and taking
Attack and defend

FORWARD
Clever ball wizard
Eyes in the back of his head
Finishing the job

REFEREES
Assuring safe flow
The buck has to stop somewhere
Correct most often

COACH
Good one too stoic
Bad one too emotional
Great one in between

FANS
Cheering their side
No matter what the result
Singing their anthem

HOOLIGANS
Hooliganism
Destructive and disruptive
No place in the game

MORE HAIKUS

MOM
Put all others first
Liberated and at home
Spiritual guide

DAD
Hard working and true
Setting a good example
His song in my soul

TOM
Hero to begin
Triumph and adversity
Hero to the end

DAN
A grasp of the world
Independent tenacious
Pragmatic all ways

JENIFER LYN
Fending for herself
Achieving and advancing
A self-made success

AMITY CHARMAINE
Deep dark peaceful calm
Erupting so silently
Goodbye little girl

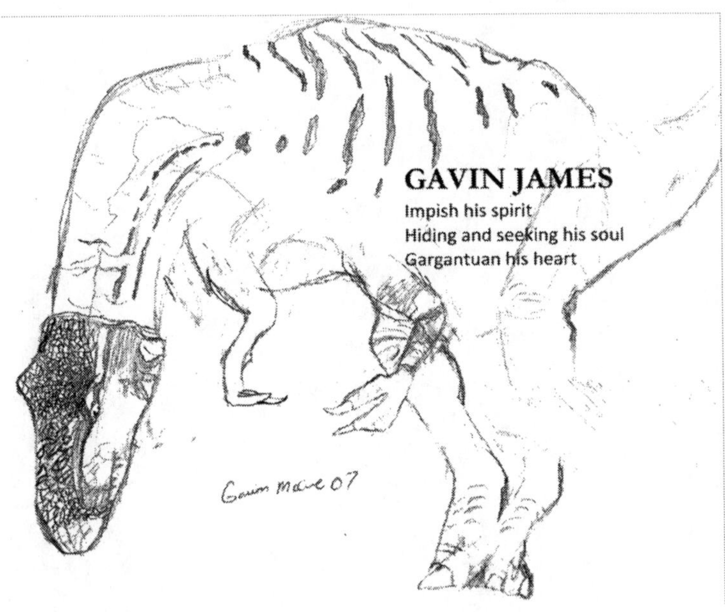
GAVIN JAMES
Impish his spirit
Hiding and seeking his soul
Gargantuan his heart

AMITY

Wonder what she thinks
Not the best father ever
Daddy, want to swim?

GAVIN

Ice cream thrown to floor
Poor Daddy is very sad
It's all right Daddy

DAN LARRIGAN
We've been through it all
Ups and downs women and war
My best friend ever

CATHY DUNN
Tumultuous times
She and I free and sassy
Healing each other

JUDY GRAGNANI
Our day didn't come
Ruby and the Romantics
'Cause her mom said so

THE NURSE
Lady with the lamp
Nancy Jenifer and Barb
Songs of nightingale

BARB ODAY
The first one ever
Rock and roll with Barbra Ann
Too fast to hold on

JUDY GRIMES
Solid and steady
With an occasional slip
Dancing on tables

CONNIE WHEELER
A wonderful source
The grass is greener seeker
Not a bad gal

JUDI WINKLER
Ruffle no feather
Modest usually right
Must get along now

HAPPY ANNIVERSARY

No one can write your married life.
For only you two
Feel the stroke of its unique rhythm,
And only you two
Are tuned to the ring of its rhyme,
But, as with all good poetry
Viewed at a glance,
These basic mechanics are lost
In the overall beauty.

AHE
ARN
06

Goodbye Florida… Hello Wherever!

ENCORE

FOUR NEW POEMS
BY JOHN McCUE

MY CUP OF TEA

I like my tea. Really, I do.
But I like it carefully brewed,
Soured, sweetened, and cooled.

I like to sip slowly. Don't you?
No need to Rush
Our tongues to be ruled.

I like tea parties. Really, I do.
Whether in Wonderland
Or Boston's Who's Who.

I don't like lies. Do you?
By chalk wielding charlatans
Who deem we need schooled.

I don't like wars. Do you?
Millions are dead
Since we have been fooled.

I like the First Amendment. Don't you?
Then please tell me why
Our anchors are pooled.

I want peace. Don't you?
I've been to war.
Have you?

THE MAD MARSUPIAL

Poor Piglet, down more by the hour,
Cried, "Rabbit, Roo's mother did sour!"
Got Kanga to retort
"Pooh, this is MY davenport!"
And her grumpiness did make the bear cower.

So the marsupial, cranky at best,
Put all of Pooh's patience to test.
"Oh, bother," said Pooh,
"What shall I do?
I've a grouch with a pouch on my couch."

ANGEVILS

We're devils and angels. We're all in cahoots.
Our fathers and mothers sprang from the same roots—
From deep down in the ocean, way up in the sky.
We'll live on forever. You'll wither and die.

Your fields are empty, and your bars are filled.
The whole world could survive on what you've spilled.
Like it or not, it's been dumped in your laps.
So, square up your shoulders, adjust those straps.

The bottles at the bar are rarin' to go
Just like the bull at the rodeo.
So, jump on that barstool. Take your best shot.
Ride 'em high, big boy! Show us what you got.

Step right on in, sir, and get some new wheels.
A test ride'll show you just how it feels.
Buy you a big one that burns ethyl gas.
Show all the ladies you got lotsa class.

Hurry up, ladies, and get your implants.
Tuck that tummy. Cram booty in your pants.
Swap integrity so you can look hot.
You'll hook you a big carp, likely as not.

Pull in that stomach! Stick out that chest!
Show us you're one of the brightest and best.
Never mind Jesus. It's alright to kill.
We'll rule the world and stick your kids with the bill.

We're angels and devils. We're all in cahoots.
Our mothers and fathers sprang from the same roots—
From deep down in the ocean, way up in the sky.
We'll live on forever. You'll wither and die.

DUST OFF

You're gonna be OK!
I'm still right here.
And here is where I'll stay
Until you no longer need me
And you're safely on your way.

I'm so thankful to you
For serving others
With courage shown by few.
Now I will stay here by your side
Until you are safely through.

You'll soon be shown the way
Through rolling meadows—
You'll find your pals and play.
Forgiveness will be forever
As there dawns a brand new day.

So rest your weary head.
We are together—
Connected human thread.
After you let me go you'll sleep—
Waking to the smell of bread.

Made in the USA
Charleston, SC
14 February 2013